Ten P(
about C

ex libris

Candlestick Press

Published by:
Candlestick Press,
Diversity House, 72 Nottingham Road, Arnold, Nottingham NG5 6LF
www.candlestickpress.co.uk

Design and typesetting by Diversity Creative Marketing Solutions Ltd.,
www.diversity.agency

Printed by Ratcliff & Roper Print Group, Nottinghamshire, UK

Selection and Introduction © John Lucas, 2016

Cover illustration: Engraving of cricketer Fuller Pilch, c.1850

Candlestick Press monogram © Barbara Shaw, 2008

© Candlestick Press, 2016

First Published 2016
Reprinted 2019

ISBN 978 1 907598 39 5

Acknowledgements:

Our thanks to John Lucas for selecting and introducing the poems.
His poem 'Still Going Strong' first appeared in *On the Track* (Redbeck Press,
2000). Thanks also to Adrian Buckner and Five Leaves Publications for
permission to reprint 'Cricket at Thrumpton' from *Contains Mild Peril* (Five
Leaves Publications, 2008). Joan Downar, 'Village Cricket' first appeared
in *Empire of Light* (Peterloo Poets, 1984) and Matt Merritt, 'Two Orthodox
Left-Armers' was first printed in *The Nightwatchman* and is reprinted here
by kind permission of the author. Hubert Moore, 'At the Cricket' is from *The
Hearing Room* (Shoestring Press, 2006) and is reprinted by kind permission of
the publisher, as is Brian Jones, 'Near Greenford, 1951' published in *New &
Selected Poems* (Shoestring Press, 2013). 'The Roller in the Woods' from *Ode to
Didcot Power Station* (Bloodaxe Books, 2014) is © Kit Wright and reprinted by
permission of the publisher. Norman Nicholson, 'Old Man at a Cricket Match'
from *A Local Habitation* (Faber & Faber, 1972) is reprinted by permission
of David Higham Associates. Our thanks to HarperCollins (Australia) for
permission to reprint Philip Hodgins, 'The Practice Nets' from *Selected
Poems* (Angus & Robertson, Sydney, 1997). Thanks also to Timothy Arlott
for permission to reprint John Arlott, 'To John Berry Hobbs on his Seventieth
Birthday'.

While every effort has been made to secure permission to reprint material
protected by copyright, we will be pleased to make good any omissions brought
to our attention in future printings of this pamphlet.

Where poets are no longer living, their dates are given.

Contents   Page

Introduction

Ten poems about cricket? Given the number of good poets who have written about the game, to choose a mere ten is mission impossible. Anyone at all familiar with cricketing poems will spot absent favourites, though since the best known are almost certainly inscribed in memory, I feel less guilty about omitting – say – Francis Thompson's 'At Lord's' than I do about other, perhaps less celebrated poems. These include Allan Ross's cameos of three great batsmen, Walter Hammond, Len Hutton and, late in his career, David Gower, recorded with affectionate wit – "the slight/ Lopsided air of a seabird/ Caught in an oilslick"; as well as Prowse's mid-nineteenth century Elegy for the great Kent all-rounder, Alfred Mynn and Gavin Ewart's 'Sadness of Cricket', both of them wonderful but, I regret to say, too long for inclusion in the present work.

Because the cricket season begins in spring and ends in early autumn, because close of play coincides with the drawing down of light, and given that the pace of the game, its many pauses, for lunch, for tea, between overs, between departing and arriving batsmen, invites prolonged conversation among spectators who are unfailingly drawn to compare the scene before them with ones chosen from the past, 'the summer game' inevitably lends itself to reminiscence, to eulogy and elegy. To a large extent, one larger than with any other sport, the meaning of cricket is in its history. It makes heroes, and occasional villains, of those cricketers gone before. Hence John Arlott's lovely tribute to Jack Hobbs on the great batsman's 70th birthday and Matt Merritt's tributes to the equally great left-arm bowlers, Wilfrid Rhodes and Hedley Verity.

But the fact that the game is associated with sunlight and wide stretches of grass brings it within reach of a kind of mistily fixed pastoral. It is easy to see how cricket, in England at least, can then be regarded as an essential expression of 'Englishness', rooted, unchanging, a land of squires and contented peasantry, of Gentlemen and Players, village cricket, village Hampdens. Nostalgia is the besetting sin of many who write about cricket.

Among the poems that follow are ones by Hubert Moore and Norman Nicholson that challenge this view while acknowledging its hold.

The Australian poet, Philip Hodgins, not only challenges simple heroics, he even invokes the word 'anatiferous' to suggest a kind of self-willed 'iron man' macho quality which perhaps many cricketers, even the least competent, dream of possessing, whether facing the fastest of bowlers or crouching in the most impossible of fielding positions. And given that the word as originally coined by Sir Thomas Browne meant "producing barnacles", Hodgins probably also has in mind certain batsmen - "Slasher" Mackay, Ken Barrington - whose sticking power is, as the saying goes, enough to break a bowler's heart. On the other hand, Brian Jones' poem beautifully evokes the uniquely testing, teasing absorption that is often experienced between batsman and bowler at any level at which the game is played.

There is also a place for irreverence. In 'Commentary', Gavin Ewart reflected that "The best thing about cricket on the radio/ is that you can shout at Trueman / at the top of your voice:/ 'You moombling, boombling, big-'eaded North country twit!'/ and he won't come round and thump you!" An altogether slyer irreverence, one offset by genuine regard, is implicit in the poems of Adrian Buckner and Joan Downar who may, by charmed coincidence, have had the same scene in mind in their depictions of village cricket, given that the latter lived in Thrumpton, where Buckner's poem is set.

But something more demanding than irreverence is needed in the face of the sheer awfulness of the cricketing establishment, which, within living memory, not only treated professional cricketers with slovenly disregard but, in its odious behaviour to Basil D'Oliveira, made plain that it saw nothing wrong in Apartheid.

This, too, is part of cricket's history. Hence, Kit Wright's excoriating 'I Found South African Breweries Most Hospitable'. ("Electrodes wired to their brains they should have had helmets,/ Balls wired up they should have been wearing a box"). The only reason the poem isn't here is that I wanted to include the same poet's 'The Roller in the Woods', which seems to me quite possibly the best poem about cricket ever written.

John Lucas

**To John Berry Hobbs on his Seventieth Birthday,
16 December 1952**

There falls across this one December day
The light remembered from those suns of June
That you reflected in the summer play
Of perfect strokes across the afternoon.

No yeoman ever walked his household land
More sure of step or more secure of lease
Than you, accustomed and unhurried, trod
Your great, but little manor, of the crease.

The game the Wealden rustics handed down
Through growing skill became, in you, a part
Of sense, and ripened to a skill that showed
Their country sport matured to balanced art.

There was a wisdom so informed your bat
To understanding of the bowler's trade
That each resource of strength or skill he used
Seemed but the context of the stroke you played.

The Master: records prove the title good.
Yet figures fail you, for they cannot say
How many men whose names you never knew
Are proud to tell their sons they saw you play.

They share the sunlight of your summer day
Of thirty years; and they, with you, recall
How, through those well-wrought centuries, your hand
Reshaped the history of bat and ball.

John Arlott (1914 – 1991)

Cricket at Thrumpton

Lined up behind boundary flags
a fleet of Renault, Nissan and Ford;
only one or two from the village now
close enough to pedal or walk.

One of the old hands regrets the lack
nowadays of spectating wives and kids –
"Folk just don't have the time – always
something else they'll need or find to do."

The midday heat unfurls across a balmy
late afternoon – what fades for an hour or two
is the significance of change – absorbed
like tomorrow's heat into a reddening sky.

Long past the casting of the die, the game
ambles on without a trace of impatience;
courtesies are exchanged between men of sixteen
and sixty, a little light applause

for a manful effort at an impossible catch.
Something, eroding perhaps, is being passed on
as an unseen cow lumbers over to chew
the wing mirror of the fast bowler's Mondeo.

Adrian Buckner

Village Cricket

On the church green, white figures
cross and re-cross in a scrupulous dance.
One clasps tenderly a ball, rolling
it in his groin. One watches from the fence
two men with staves who seem to be leaders
striking the sacred soil. As if in a trance
they crouch. The ball is loosed, is struck, falling
impotently to one who hitches up his pants.

Grass burns green fire; like flames
the white men flicker, fumble all the bright
afternoon. One in a dairy coat tames
wild cries with a blessing, as tight
to the boundary cattle crowd, and the ball claims
all its victims in the summer rite.

Joan Downar (1930 – 1996)

The Practice Nets

The way a dream of sporting glory dissolves
when early morning light seeps grimly back
into the room, so too this half-constructed aviary
with its slabs of wire mesh and concrete floor.
Instead of dirty Tipp-Ex worms the droppings
are red-raw skid marks mostly in the middle
where some of the unhelmeted batsmen lost sight
of just the ball they needed to keep an eye on.
Their bats are like the pitch in miniature.
Each one is badly scarred with the hot spots
and rashes of that disease which spreads beyond
the playing victims to their wives and kids –
the sempiternal pain of a middle-order collapse.
But perhaps worse are those more personal wounds:
the split webbing after a dropped slips catch,
two broken toes from practising in sandshoes,
and everyman's nightmare of turning full-on
to an awkward ball without the vital box.
When banishment from next week's team is likely
the anatiferous number-three will come back
to this uncovered nave and go through strokes
with all the devotion of a former sinner.
Watching the one who used to be their idol
groups of schoolchildren will hang along the aisles,
their fingers poking dangerously through the wire.
An act of public penitence is always fraught.
The padded man who finds himself exposed
to such a swaying congregation is never sure
which ball is going to cut sharply off the seam.
The only choice is to practise a straight bat
as if the life of chance could be theorized.

Not that these children pushing against wire
would ever be impressed with a return to form
which only happened before the five real days.
They know that that's the attraction of the nets.
It doesn't matter how many times you're out.
You'll always carry your bat. It's like a dream.

Philip Hodgins (1959 – 1995)

Near Greenford, 1951

Like a vision it was unaccountable.
I parted branches and there it was,
totally absorbed with itself.
In old cream, with a fringed baldness,

the bowler six times looped a slow ball
like a deeply considered question,
and six times the batsman in his plum cap
leaned very attentively and returned an answer.

Six times. And time did not matter,
was utterly elsewhere.
There were fielders listening
and distant waiting batsmen in shadow

under trees listening. It was like staring
into deep water
at unexplained subtleties of light.
I was achingly excluded in another element.

Though I found my way back
it was never back to that:
perfect exposition, perfect refutation,
and something beyond them both, winning.

Brian Jones (1938 – 2009)

Still Going Strong

Past 70, Joe Hardstaff's
weather-veined eyes stared
to where he'd flicked my question
over the boundary board.

"The fastest bowler? Lol!*
Any time, when he'd done,
even in the nets,
your shirt-tail had some brown."

A Woodbine-tangled laugh,
then cardiganed shoulders swivelled
suddenly, wrists snapped up
to grip an imagined handle

and Joe modelled Stillness
before lips curved in a sweet
just-so smile as the ball
dropped safely by his feet.

John Lucas

* "Lol" Harold Larwood (1904 – 1995), Notts. and England fast
bowler.

Two Orthodox Left-Armers

I. Wilfrid Rhodes (1877 – 1973)

"Tha' can't put in what God left out."
Heaven sent, then, those few short strides,
an unwavering rhythm, and the loose, lovely arc
of the arm. A trajectory looping from Golden Age

to Bradman. And being White Rose born and bred,
never was a legacy better spent. Every ball an interrogation,
every over a conspiracy of art and science.
But land a ball on a sixpence?

"Nay, lad, I can hit a newspaper, spread reight out
at that, and if the batsman thinks as I'm spinning it
then I am."

II. Hedley Verity (1905 – 1943)*

"He'll do," said Wilfrid. No higher praise,
unless it's this. The Don, run-glutted in a summer
of rewriting Wisden yet again, but still struggling to master
the high, easy action and scrupulous control
in the face of every onslaught. "You see,
there's no breaking point with him."

Or maybe this. Shell-bursts, a net of tracers closing fast,
but as upright among blazing Sicilian corn
as on any Scarborough dog day. And still no question
but to "keep going, keep going"
to every limit, and beyond.

Matt Merritt

* Hedley Verity was killed in the Sicilian landings in WWII.